Contents

Introduction

I first wrote these short essays between the ages of ten and twelve, in the years 2012-2015. I have kept most of them as I have grown older and refined my approach to the topics discussed in the book. I wanted to capture my thoughts and feelings in this critical period of life, where the thoughts came before the actions. I am now twenty three years old, the time of life when the actions and the thoughts happen at the same time. I hope these essays give some insight into the thought process of an overthinking, pubescent kid trying to think his way through the world.

About the Author

Aidan O'Nan is the author of Thoughts Before Actions (2025), which is his debut published work. He is based in Indianapolis, where he lives with his family. When he's not writing, he can be found designing civil engineering projects, exercising, or reading.

Society

One of the greatest debates in our world is one of perspective. What are we, as a species, being, entity, soul? Has the revolution into the Information Age changed us for the better? While some think it has turned us into a better world, others say it holds a dark future.

The society we live in is top-class, and it's never going back. With globalization, information can be anywhere, anytime. Someone in Bangkok can catch up on what their friend is doing in Chicago! It can raise awareness for a little boy in London who has cancer. Nothing gets around faster than computer signals connecting throughout the world. And with this, our society will progress faster than ever.

Our launch into the stars will progress us even more. A multitude of space programs are aiming for Mars and other objects. Soon, life will be above our heads and into the clouds, thus discovering more than ever. They say that Space is the "final frontier". The West is not even close to the vastness and multitude of outer space. Colonizing other planets and eventually out of our galaxy.

On the other hand, our society is going six feet under. Pollution, crime, and general gluminess is turning our world down. The failure of our own might well destroy us before we reach the stars, or maybe before anything else worthwhile. The Avengers series likes to indirectly mention this. While others may ignore it, it will become a major part of life in the foreseeable future.

Us as human beings do some pretty stupid stuff. And sooner or later, someone pretty stupid is running the world. Maybe someone already is. The direction these "leaders" are taking us is not for the better of the common people. With much of humanity's faith already lost, we have no choice but to either believe in the nonsense of religion or plunge ourselves into the darkness that the government takes us.

So what really is society? While some may believe it is a diamond in the rough, others argue it is turning into a black hole. Both sides present convincing arguments. And only time can tell the outcome. But remember, whether you keep optimism and faith or not is up to You.

Family

At the beginning of your life, you have a mom. There are many like it, but this one is yours. A mom should give you affection, love, and be tasked with the responsibility of raising you. You may also have a dad. This guy is your mom's partner, helping her with the stuff mom can't do. There is also a chance you have a sibling or more than one. These people are going through the same thing you are, only they have different experiences or going through different stages. Your family may also have a pet.

Throughout your childhood, your family helps you understand social, physical, and developmental concepts of everyday life. Combine that with school, and you're learning almost everything you need to become an adult. Your siblings may also teach you to be nice (or mean) to other people.

When you become an adult, hard times may come upon you. And even if you are a successful lawyer or a cashier, family is all that we truly have. They are the only people who you truly got, and without them, we can't go on. So whether you are sick, or just got fired, there

is no better place to get help than your family.
Your parents will no doubt let you be helped
back on your feet again.

When you get older, you may get married and
have kids. Through this process, you are
making a family of your own. By having a child
you are giving them a window of opportunity.
An opportunity into a lifetime of wonder, joy,
and many other experiences. And without you,
they can't go on in their lives as well. They need
you to survive, just like you and your parents.

At the end of the day, your family is the most
important relationship you have, and you need
them to raise you into something beautiful.
Remember to love your parents, siblings, and
pets, because the stuff they did to you shaped
you into the person you are.

God

The term God has been referred to as someone with omnipotent power. Someone who has the power to help or harm our world. Throughout human history, we have built monuments, fought wars, and made religion a way of life. This is the way Gods affects our world and everyday life. However, though the ultimate God comes in many different shapes and forms, the question that has needed answering for a long time is: Is there a God?

If God created the universe, then surely he would have given us the good fortune of making contact with extraterrestrial life. Why would he force wars upon us? It is highly unlikely that his life was recorded so accurately, especially since most other data back then wasn't clear. Also a lot of us would have the same power God had, since Jesus had him. If anything, God sounds like a good dictator, though unreal.

Though God seems like a good person, he and his legacy seem false to me. If he does things that no other human can do, does that make him alien? People generally do not trust other-world creatures. And why do millions of people want to follow him thousands of years after his death?

One good thing God has done is save lives. Because many people know him, they turn to him, potentially saving countless suicides. It also connects people on Sunday. But other than that, most of the things he tells us in the Bible are hard to believe. Though it could be possible that he may have existed, his descendants would have similar powers, and we don't see that in our world today. Plus, scientists are saying that God's presence in the universe is becoming less likely.

At the end of the day, whether you're Presbyterian, Jewish, or something else, the legends of an omnipotent person doing good for the world isn't true. While I think it does some good, the practices and policies are simply not true.

Photography

Some think that photography is just picture with no real meaning or importance. However, photos are the visual archives of the universe around us. Some photography can be a selfie, marking how good you looked that day. Other photography is by using satellites, finding far away planets with the potential of supporting human life. Whatever the occasion, photography has connected and progressed our world and how we see others.

The average photo-taker can still have photos be a big part of their lives. Selfies can help remember meeting friends. Taking pictures of food can respark how good a meal was. Pictures of vacations, pets, family, and anything in between can keep memories of what you did and when you did it. Plus, you can share these photos so others can see as well.

Professional photography is another aspect of the photo world. People make a living travelling to the farthest places to get a picture of the best landscape. Other people take photos of current events, snapping pictures of an ongoing war or covering the President making a speech. However they want to, professional photographers strive to capture our world in a different light than most others do.

With Outer Space becoming a new frontier, pictures of the new West have become important for discovering new features. Scientists and researchers are taking advantage of the cameras on their probes and satellites. The detail and range on some photos now are unimaginable from what some thought possible from the Space Race era. Many new people are joining and becoming engaged via social media, watching and helping explorers explore the unknown.

Before cameras were around, portrait painters and people who drew historical battles were photographers. Cavemen, who drew the simplest things can be considered pictures as well. When cameras first came out, it took a little imagination to see beauty, for there was no color. However, as more advanced technology came around, it has become easier to see the world, the stars, and selfies through globalization.

Whether it is a simple photo of your dog or documenting the outer reaches of the world, photography is a way to connect, share, inspire,

and catch a glimpse into the universe around,
agave, and below us.

Seasons

A long time ago, when humans were very primitive and hunted for a living, most activities were decided by the weather. If it was winter, your food may have been hibernating. Like it does today, the seasons determined what clothes you wore. However, this piece will focus on the representational meaning of the seasons. What it feels like, what it means, and what you can do.

Spring. After a cold, unforgiving winter, the morning dew of grass is followed by blooming flowers. The temperature increases, giving off a nice warm feeling along with the sight of kids beginning to play again. The feeling of life seeps back into the landscape. It is only the beginning of a series of beautiful seasons.

Summer. After a nice spring, the temperatures and humidity continue to increase until it's uncomfortable. Insects, animals, and other things are abuzz. So many festivals, cookouts, and other outdoor activities happen here. It is as if the content level for everyone is at its peak. The serenity of the weather outside relaxes everyone. As long as the heat stays under control, everything is as it should be.

Fall. School starts as the outdoors becomes more random. The humid rain or the foggy wind starts to occur. The fun holiday of Halloween gets us in the proper Fall mood. Not to mention the beautiful transformation of trees. The leaves turn dull shades and fall off, making the season even more fun. The beverages of Fall also flourish during this time. The fun never seems to end as the seasons ever-change.

Winter. The snow flowers down as the coldest season comes around. This makes for a fun environment for playing. Everyone adopts a huddled lifestyle to cope with the temperature drop. The Holidays of Thanksgiving and Christmas enhance the feeling of happiness. The New Year marks the new, fresh start of another set of seasons.

Though friends, family, and other variables may change, you can almost always count on the weather to be joyful, fun, and a great experience.

Stories

Everyone has a story. Everyone can make a story. People tell, write, and act out stories. People can make a living writing or acting out stories. If you think about it, everyTHING has a story. Where it was, where it went, what it does. Unfortunately, most things aren't alive to tell the story. Awards programs give prizes to the best movies, songs, books, and other things that have the most qualified stories in a specific category. If you look at it, everything is just a story, history being made.

If we start with living beings, they have the ability to share their stories. Like me. I'm just a 12 year old boy who lives in Indiana and writing about stories. And my mom has a story as well. She was born and raised in the Soviet Union. See? Everyone has a story. Whether they choose to share it or not is their choice.

Things like single molecules have stories as well. Where they are, what they are in, what they are used for. Other structures such as planets have history as well. These objects cannot tell stories, but living things can tell their stories for them. There are also things that are not living, but were made to tell their own story. The ways to tell a story about a non-living thing can be infinite.

Story telling in our world is a big industry. People who are authors, photographers, and other jobs tell stories about everything. You could say a librarian is a protector of stories. Sometimes if a book is popular enough, it can get turned into a movie, which is another way of telling a story. If you look around, people make stories about faraway places, impossible things, and plots that can only be real inside their heads.

The stories around us define our environment and how it may react to our presence. With all of this history around us, we can predict what they went through in the past. Stories are simply everything.

Music

Sound. One of the fundamental concepts in our lives, and perhaps the universe. Most species on our planet have been able to conquer sound in order to communicate. Humans are the only species that makes sound to entertain. Even more odd, humans are the only species that pay to live on Earth. One way we can get money is by creating sounds, either through our thoughts or by making contact with another object.

One of the greatest things about music is that it can evoke memory, emotion, and connection. Spotify is the leading organization that strives for emotion. Music festivals like Bonnaroo establish connection. Shakespeare's iambic pentameter that he used to create great plays is what most artists do now to create the best sounding music.

Surprisingly, the science behind sound and music is simple. Most songs have a beat, and you can create a beat by tapping on almost anything. Humans tend toward a 4-beat measure. From then on, we have mastered woodwinds, strings, and just recently, digital instruments. DJs have become very popular for

the intense, heart-pounding rhythm they
provide.

Sound is one of the most basic concepts for human insight. And in recent years, it has turned into a billion dollar industry. People who make sounds that are so beautiful and catchy can become billionaires themselves. But for those who don't make music professionally, it is so simple to create a basic tune that we take the privilege for granted. One of the biggest benefits is that it connects us. Through manipulating our mouths, we can communicate efficiently. In closing, the effects of sound and music are extremely beneficial to our everyday lives.

Density Fluctuations

When the Big Bang occurred, the fate of the universe was considered chaotic and irregular. If one believes that there is more than one universe, some universes must then be uniform and orderly, at least according to the Infinite Probabilities Theory. When a universe becomes chaotic, density fluctuations are the main reason the planets, stars, and other things exist. As of now, no one knows the cause of the uneven universe, even though during the early expansion, it has largely smoothed out.

Even in the chaotic world we live in, our universe is still subject to entropy. In a long time, the universe will even out, and nothing will exist. Uniform universes, I believe, are already in a maximum state of entropy, without the development of time. Though there is time and space, the density of the universe is even everywhere. There are no stars, black holes, life, anything. One example of entropy is the uniform radiation in every direction throughout the universe.

What does this mean for us? We are lucky that the chance universe we were thrown into has different densities. But on Earth, our daily lives are affected by this principle in the form of weather. Thunderstorms are the effect of a massive pressure difference in the atmosphere. However, the air pressure on Earth is naturally trying to balance itself out, only creating more weather. This is good, because without weather there are no plants, no life on land, no us. But what if, for some miraculous reason, the density and air pressure has evened all around Earth? The answer is that that won't happen. There's too many variables to compensate for. The Earth's tectonic plates shift in elevation and we build things that change the composition of the corresponding air column. We can always expect the rain to be there until something catastrophic happens.

Entropy itself is an unavoidable concept, at least in this universe. Without entropy, a latte macchiato can stay in its layers while you sip on it on your way to work. Eventually, it is likely that our universe could become uniform. After a long time, the clouds that form stars become exhausted and decay into nothing.

In the end, the chaos that occurs, whether it be planets or black holes, is one of the biggest deciding factors for life and density fluctuations as we know it.

Social Media

On the main shelf on my iPhone, I have social media apps as 3 out of the 4 apps. Instagram, YouTube, Camera (for selfies), and Google. I will use Instagram as my prime example for this piece. Social media has the power to connect, inspire, and enjoy others' moments. On the downside, jealousy, piracy, and other bad things can come as a result of this new trend.

Social media's greatest benefit is globalization. It allows someone from Manila to see what their friend in New York City is doing. Everyone who has an Instagram can access millions of profiles and get a glimpse into their life. The invention of hashtags have further helped direct and connect people from different backgrounds into a single subject or topic.

Another pro of social media is the evocative aspect. Seeing or hearing about others' experience can help, create, inspire, and love yourself. The emotions that strike your body when you read or see something joyful or tragic are beautiful. After all, it is one of the best things humans can do.

With everything, there is an opposite to this emerging trend. Social media has become a main cause of low self-esteem. Many users of social media have rendered themselves worthless because they don't get likes or followers. This has created a caste system in schools, communities, and other places. After all, the concept of social media is to connect and create, not destroy.

Supporting the previous evidence is the piracy concept of social media. Through access to people's profiles, stalkers and predators can do what they do easier than ever. These people can find where you live through advanced technology. Through social media, you are placing you, your friends, family, and school in danger. By taking pictures and posting them while out of town, people can easily break into your house.

Zero Energy

Why can we move? We consume energy in order to use it. But where does all this energy come from? All the things we see come from the energy of the Big Bang. But where did the Big Bang get its energy? Whether the energy came from a god, or spontaneous loss of entropy, the energy had to come from somewhere.

The answer is surprisingly easy: none. The total energy in the universe is exactly zero. The principle of antiparticles and negative gravitational attraction balance out all energy to zero. If there is no total energy, why was there a Big Bang? Why are we here?

What made the Big Bang? If the energy balance was and still is equal, then why was there a need to create time and space? The following is a list of possible solutions, though there are more.

1. The creation of the universe was an act of God. I personally don't believe in God, but I am rather referring to him as an outside force, a being outside our world and beyond our comprehension. Its need

to create us, use us, and possibly manipulate us is unknown. I doubt this reason highly for I think this God would steer me away from writing this very sentence.

2. Perhaps the universe was nothing, but then because of its infinite mass and density, the universe "exploded" at a certain point (0,0,0) and started time and space. I believe that the simultaneous loss of entropy is responsible for this way of Creation.

3. This possibility is unlikely, but if there was never any total energy in the universe, then there was never a reason for the Big Bang. Instead, the universe is infinite in time. No "Beginning" or "Time 0". That way the universe has no reason for needing to release energy, but instead it has always been there.

Nature

The Earth started out as a hot rock with no atmosphere and tons of volcanoes. Over millions of years, the atmosphere developed and water came to Earth in the form of meteors. These are the building blocks for life on Earth. These single-cell organisms evolved to live on land, and eventually monkeys evolved to create homo sapiens, which are the first kind of humans.

Though we are from nature, our need for resources and infrastructure have destroyed lots of natural habitats and forced extinction upon many species of animals. However, efforts from organizations have influenced people and governments to recycle, stop global warming, and protect animals. The trees of the world are getting chopped down. Trees. As they reach high in the sky, they get cut down. The trees and grass and bushes are the most common part of nature.

The trees on mountains are -in my opinion- one of the most beautiful things there are. The ugly chainsaws and cutters are destroying these beautiful landscapes. They then become concrete. Buildings, offices, and homes become of what was once trees. The one reason: Greed. Wealthy people and corporations want more land to house more people and make more money. The money is all that some people want.

Though the environment appears to be getting destroyed, we are doing things to help. Recycling rates have quadrupled over the four basic recyclables. The reuse of recyclable materials has saved millions of trees over the past thirty years. The amount of landfills that have been infected with materials that could have been refilled is insane.

The fact that humans are destroying our own home can be startling. But the innovation and intelligence of people around the globe are creating frugal ways to carry out everyday tasks. I predict that in the next thirty years, people around the world will create a greener, brighter, and better tomorrow.

Parallel

The universe is what we live in. Everything we say, think, and do is contained within the universe. Except for the thought of other universes. There is an ongoing debate of whether the universe is spatially infinite or there are infinite universes. If there are other worlds, then these are called parallel universes. However, there is one slight difference. The timeline of another universe is different. Hitler won WWII, for example. Because there are infinite universes, there are infinite timelines.

The timelines of all universes can be anything, literally. Because of this, we are very fortunate to live in an extremely peaceful timeline. In another universe, the Earth suddenly disappears as I am writing this sentence. The fact that this timeline has intelligent life asking these questions is really a miracle.

The incredible thing about infinite universes is that anything – and I mean anything – can be changed and is possible. Even just by an atom, it can be changed and still end up completely differently. That's the beauty of us; move in one different way and perhaps the whole world could change, either for better or for worse.

How that's possible, no one knows. And no one may ever know.

I know what you're thinking: "If the timelines have already been done, then what's the point of doing anything at all?" Well, we don't know. We could be in the universe where if something happens, the other thing will happen in another scenario and break off. All universes could be paired with their exact opposite, maybe.

From the beginning of time, the possibilities of differences are endless. And though we may be one of infinite, our uniqueness in our world is unmatched and more natural than we could ever possibly imagine.

Movies

The screen that plays it all. From sci-fi to horror, people can't get enough of the dark room, bag of popcorn, and a good movie. However, I think movies have a deeper meaning than the suspense or adrenaline. They have a way of connecting us. The movies that come out now teach almost every cardinal moral. Through these stories, the movie craze has us learning better and defeating evil for the better of mankind.

Fiction has produced some of the best films in history. Though all works of fiction are possible, battles on other galaxies or giant lizards never fail to amaze us. The feeling of something supernatural happening right before our eyes is something most everyday situations won't get you. With new technology enhancing the audio and visual aspects of the modern theater, these stories look as realistic as ever.

As much as we like fiction, nonfiction is just as exciting. Movies such as "Nonstop" and "127 Hours" give an insight to what it would be like for a modern-day thriller to appear in our world. It could also give horrifying nightmares if it were real. Soon, as we reach for the stars, the space stories that we show on screen may soon become real. Whether it be an adventure or a horror, it is sure to happen soon at this current rate.

In the 1960s, the first movies with color and sound appeared. Before that, it took an imagination to enjoy the movie experience. Without sound or color, some movies were trapped without audio or correct visuals. Back then, it took a lot of work to incorporate color into flicks. Now it is included. In some special theaters, there are 4D or even 5D effects. 3D enhanced the movie experience greatly.

Whether it is superheroes fighting supernatural threats or killers on the loose, the thrill of movies will never cease to keep us on the edge of our seat. And at the current rate, the new technologies of the latest cinema will make future movies better than ever.

Communication

In today's society, technology has the goal of connecting everyone to everything. This is the first time a Snapchat from a girl in Sydney can be received by her friend in London in a matter of seconds. In fact, today's technology can disrupt families from talking at meals because they are texting a friend or colleague. However, throughout history, connectivity was very primitive and could take years to receive a letter.

When language was simply nonsense stranded together in the most recent Ice Age, communication was crucial. Deciding where to hunt took no words to figure out. The body language, eye contact, and motions were the only form of connecting with your tribe. The Egyptians were smart in creating visual patterns to create a successful language. In today's world, the so-called "Steps of Civilization" include language, a proper and quick way of communicating.

However, as time went on, people began to group sounds with symbols, and those symbols put together create a certain pattern of noises. They are then put together with anything, literally. Thus, the first languages were formed. These started popping up all over the world, each one usually paired with a culture or tribe. Now an American from Korea may speak fluent Korean but hardly know any English. In fact, language is so important that it is considered one of the six steps to beginning a civilization.

Once we mastered language, new forms started to appear. These came in the form of code. Computers and electronic systems can now communicate all over the world. With a region of connectivity opening up, the process of globalization sped up dramatically. Smartphones, apps, and websites are just a portion of what has become of the latest revolution in communication.

In schools, communication is seen as a crucial skill to teach kids. In the workplace, teamwork through communication is being reinforced as well. If the human race went about ignoring each other, then nothing would ever get done. Through thousands of years, hundreds upon hundreds of languages have popped up for all kinds of purposes. Though many languages go extinct, all languages will be remembered as one of the most essential parts of life.

Books

The environment surrounding us is often filled with nonsensical things, shapes, objects. But around 3200 BC sparked one of the biggest changes in human history. It's what makes you able to read this and me able to write this. The invention of writing revolutionized how we see the world. It allowed us to store information without telling stories generation to generation.

The first alphabet known was created by the Phoenicians. They were smart, seafaring people who knew what they were doing. Since then, people started using their own alphabets to communicate between neighbors, villages, even oceans. Now, information can be recorded, events written down, and tragedies scribed. To put symbols on paper was something no one had ever seen or done before: to communicate without talking or drawing, but with characters people write with.

In the modern world, more and more languages are being created, mainly in the form of code. Telling computers to do things with a more advanced form of writing is expanding the limits of what we can create. Many great pieces of literature have (of course) been written. Without writing, Shakespeare, Twain, and Tolkien probably would not be or have been successful. Though it may seem a little ridiculous, be thankful for all the good books we can read and talk about.

The future of books will be more accessible for all. The rising trend of e-books and audiobooks allow people to listen to whatever, whenever. To listen to a book while driving a car has advanced multitasking to a whole new level. More information can be processed in less time.

Since the beginning of writing and text and books, our everyday life has evolved into a complex and advanced society. The beauty we scribble onto paper is a cornerstone of human knowledge. Never has a set of symbols transformed the way we remember, progress, or communicate between people. Though it is a simple concept, I hope we can all appreciate what a simple yet incredible thing it is to write.

Technology Revolution

I don't think that anyone three hundred years ago predicted a world where electronics rule. The way this entirely new concept we are living in is rapidly growing on us like a third arm. If you look around, people may actually have a digital third arm. Come and explore the impact the digital is inflicting upon us, for better or for worse.

The use of applying scientific knowledge for practical purposes can be used for many good things. The term "globalization"is becoming known because it's what is happening all around us right now. A person in New York City can chat, call, text, or play games with someone in Shanghai. Business transactions can be confirmed in the blink of an eye, even if the companies are physically located across the world. The communication approach to technology has benefited humanity in many ways.

Technology has expanded beyond screens and into the physical world. 3D-printed prosthetic arms are being made and used as I write. Algorithms are being used to calculate the stocks, the forecast, and sports outcomes better than ever. The integration of these applied sciences has made our world so simple, yet so much more complex. Even though technology has benefited us in many ways, there are plenty of negatives to counter the progress.

One of the major issues in technology is its application in conflicts, big and small. Cyberbullying is tormenting kids left and right, giving mean people another way to feel dominant. Drones, hacking, and missiles are turning heads with new ways to create damage on a worldwide scale. Globalization has made communication easier, so harsh words can be sent faster than ever. Though people try to be good, others simply can't help but take advantage of all the power they have and turn the world evil with it.

However, even with its pros and cons, technology keeps moving forward. The world seems to find more ways to use it for better than for worse. After all, I wrote two good sections in comparison to one bad. In an ideal world, these new inventions would only help, never harm. But that is not so. It has not happened in the past and there will be no exception in the future. The goods and evils of technology will live side by side for years to come.

Sports

As my mom once said, "sports are man's substitute for war". With globalization, the general sports industry has become bigger and more complex than ever. Someone in Dallas can watch the Cowboys play on their television while streaming PSG on their phone. People can also wear their team colors, having enough resources to make the right kind of fabric. Even stats can be measured to the millimeter to see if the ball passed the goal line.

While the human race is at an all-time low for wars, we are at an all-time high in sports. Many efforts that bring peace to the world through sports are succeeding. This forces people to resort to sports, one of the few legal options that can cause giant fights and rivalries. The usage of sports to cause disagreements is becoming high, but there is almost nothing we can do to prevent the love of sports.

The athletic ability of someone can now be measured more accurately than ever. Cameras, sensors, and better equipment can produce results like the line and angle a player takes to hunt down a soccer ball. Like in the previous section, people can back their arguments by using facts like how many yards or points scored. Computer technology can recognize a trend in a player's ability in, say, water polo before anyone else can. Last but not least, tennis balls can be ruled down to the hundredth of a centimeter.

In prehistoric times, a person was judged on how fast they could run or how far they could throw a spear. With proper training, people are now pushing the limits of how fast one can swim or bike. Because we don't usually judge a person by their ability to fight or hunt, we often use sports to benchmark how good he or she is.

The sports that we encounter may just be a side interest for some, but for others it is a way of life. Some people spend days watching their team lose in cricket. Others practice three sports for six hours every day. Sports are how we get physical activity, helping the body maintain a healthy lifestyle. Those that play simply to do their best, though, are the best ones of all!

Alone

The feeling. It might not seem like much to some. Others too much. Being alone isn't just being by yourself. You are with your thoughts as well. Whether being scared of loneliness affects you or not, it is still an interesting emotion. How it treats you is how you act when you're not around other people.

Some people enjoy being alone. Just yourself, no peer pressure, nobody to disagree with. Many can be much happier and more productive when there are no distractions to get in the way. Some religions focus on inner peace, and to do that while being alone is often the key. Many people in society simply like to be alone, and sometimes the product of doing that makes the person happier and do what they do better.

There is an equal downside to being alone. Sometimes the things people do during themselves can result in some destructive things. Solitude cuts people off from their normal habits and makes them crazy. The mental handicap on the lonely can make them useless, or feel a need to be wanted again, and become destructive. The damage from a lack of attention has affected many other lives as well.

Being alone isn't so dangerous as surviving alone. Being truly alone, with no outside contact, is the basis of many shows and stories. The production of these shows focuses more on the survival aspect rather than the mental obstacles. To live alone, survive alone, think alone and get through it can be a great challenge. The mental aspects of being alone can change people, and not always for the better.

The feeling. Sometimes good, sometimes not, we all have our own opinion of it. Too many times has society displayed the effects of loneliness, reminding us all that we are either beneficial or vulnerable to ourselves. Whichever one we are, use it and control it.

Age

Age is more than a number, it's a timeline. What you've done, how long you've done it. The age of all of us is always increasing, but that shouldn't slow you up. Age is not a restriction to what you can and can't do. The age of anything is simply a number, and can do anything it wants to.

When you are born, the timer starts. It sets a different amount for all of us, but it starts nonetheless. From then on, you race. As fast as you can, to get an education, a job, a spouse, children. But we never care to slow down a lot. To look at the big picture. Where we go in life can be a big deal, and the best time to do it is as soon as possible. To know where we are headed is to know our own goals in life.

As you get older and the ever-changing concept of life unfolds, restrictions and freedoms go along with it. We can't wait to get our driver's license, can't wait to drink alcohol. But when we get these privileges, we long for the days when our parents cared for us, and we could be kids again. The list of cans and cannots changes as we go on, but the time as kids is the list we should enjoy the most.

As you grow older, the capabilities of the human body start to shrink. With the new technology present and certain to come in the future, living longer and healthier is easier than ever before. Soon age won't be a problem to consider until you have existed for hundreds, maybe even thousands of years. Technology frontiers are allowing our age to be something to celebrate, not to worry about.

It has been long since dreams of computers and advanced science were only dreams. If the future holds ways to maintain your age over a long time, then the dreams are headed the right way. If the TV shows of freeze pods come true, then that is a future I want to be a part of.

Age is an interesting thing. It grows at a linear rate, yet some parts seem, and will, be slower or faster than others. And as you step back and look at the number, and the things that go with it, your age is the experienced end of what you have done, yet it is still expanding. And still expanding, and still expanding.

Future

Wait one second after reading this. That second is gone forever, lost from the universe. What did you do in that one second? What did everyone else do in that one second? The things the universe and everyone in it do seem normal at most times, but the time we have left is precious. Use it wisely.

Lives we lead. Every day the lives we use are being eaten by time. The days we waste being mean and hurting other people takes a toll on us. It needs to be better known that people should use their time to help others, do amazing things, become one-of-a-kind. With the infinite things to be interested in, there is always a way to own the future, and have fun in your life.

Futures and their contents come with time. As far as I know, the speed of light cannot be surpassed. The time we discover new things in outer space may have been billions of years gone, but the light of the object is just arriving to our eyes. Much of the history of planets has been lost from our late arrival to space discovery. The final frontier is ours as far as the eye can see, but the future of it is unpredictable.

The way we expand humankind's reach into the stars is the way we develop our future. If we follow our destiny on Earth, aggressively expand, use up resources, then the fate of mankind will diminish quickly. If we learn to use resources wisely and learn about the outer world carefully, then our race can prosper and flourish.

The future is always being talked about, always in limbo. The time we have needs to be used well, whether on the ground or in the stars. Learning to be caring to the environment around us will make you a good person. Advancing yourself and others along the way will let you live a good life.

Routine

It can come so naturally. Getting into the habit of doing something over and over again. Doing something routinely has its pros and cons. Being able to get into a habit and being productive with it can be beneficial for you and your environment. Being stuck in a routine can make things boring for you and your environment. In the end it all depends if you use a routine in the right way.

Routines are very helpful in many situations. They make day-to-day tasks easier to do. Sticking to a routine means knowing how to efficiently manage those tasks. This can increase productivity and good habits. To maintain a steady, active routine makes you work smarter and become more reliable.

Though routines can be helpful, there are many cons to adapting to one. Humans naturally fear change, so if their routines have to be changed, then said humans would get uncomfortable with the routine. Another case would be if you became so attached to doing a certain thing at a specific time that other events would be ignored. If you could not go to an event because you're doing something in that time for a while, then that is not good use of a routine.

To be in a routine not only means helping or hurting yourself, but others as well. If other people know of your times, it can get more people involved, which makes more people productive. But if others have to bend to your schedule to be with you, then that can be disrespectful. Not only do you need a routine for you, you need to know others' routines as well.

The concept of a routine is fairly simple. Just a regularly followed sequence of actions. Yet the way we use these routines can affect the routine user and those around the user. Routines create habits, and whether those habits are good or bad, it is up to you to use them well.

www.ingramcontent.com/pod-product-compliance
Lightning Source LLC
Chambersburg PA
CBHW021402160726
47994CB00007B/3048